In the Line of Fire

American Diplomats in the Trenches

Edited by

Ambassador (ret) Charles Ray

North Potomac, MD

Printed in the United States of America.

Cover Photo: Public domain image (photo by U.S. Marine Corps) of U.S. Embassy building in Beirut, Lebanon after 1983 bombing.

ISBN: 1505672724
ISBN-13: 978-1505672725

DEDICATION

Dedicated to all the valiant men and women who have gone abroad in the service of liberty and freedom as diplomatic representatives of our great country. Many have paid the supreme price for that service and have labored without notice by most of their fellow countrymen.

In the Line of Fire

CONTENTS

———————

Photograph by Charles Ray

ACKNOWLEDGMENTS

I would like to thank everyone who gave so graciously of their time to make this book possible.

First, my deepest gratitude goes to Frank Lavin, who was ambassador to Singapore when I served as ambassador to Cambodia, who has been an ardent supporter of this project from the time I came up with the idea. Thanks also go to those who provided anecdotes of their service; the late Gene Marshall for the account of his time as a junior officer in a crisis situation, Jim Maher for the description of his brief tour in Somalia, Jon Dorschner for the story of his tour in Bangladesh as the start of the first Gulf War, Mike Meszaros for the point of view of a civil service employee who also served overseas, and Colonel (retired) Dave Jesmer for the story of his time as a defense attaché during a terrorist attack in Syria.

I am most grateful to the Association of Diplomatic Studies and Training (ADST), in particular Charles Stuart Kennedy, for granting me access to their oral history archives, and giving me permission to use them. The archives are a veritable treasure trove of information about life as an American diplomat from a vast array of perspectives.

A word of appreciation to the staff and board of the American Foreign Service Association (AFSA), who maintain the Memorial Plaques which honor American diplomats who have died in service to the country.

Finally, I would like to salute all my friends and colleagues of the U.S. Foreign Service for their dedication and valor, and for the support and friendship shown to me during my 30 years in the service. I have tried to tell your story accurately.

In the Line of Fire

INTRODUCTION

Webster's New Universal Unabridged Dictionary (1983) defines **diplomacy** as 'the conducting of relations between nations, by their heads directly, or through accredited representatives; the act of managing international negotiations '. A **diplomat** is defined as 'a representative of a government who conducts relations with another government in the interests of his own country; a person whose career or profession is diplomacy.'

After serving 30 years in the U.S. Foreign Service, representing the United States as a diplomat in six countries, and serving in senior positions in the United States, I've come to the conclusion that most Americans have little understanding of what American diplomats really do.

American diplomacy has a long history, predating the founding of the republic by many years. Before the Revolutionary War, the thirteen English colonies were subject to European peace settlements, settlements with Native American tribes, and inter-colony agreements established in London, although each colony had agents stationed in London. Despite this, there inter-colonial conferences established to deal with purely local matters. It was only when relations between London and the New World colonies began to break down that Americans began to involve themselves in the conduct of diplomacy.

In the years immediately after independence, the new country was represented abroad by cultured, educated gentlemen who had strong political ties to the small ruling elite that were building the new nation. The United States did not even send ambassadors abroad until 1893, sending instead ministers - or envoys extraordinary and ministers plenipotentiary, a rank below ambassador. From the presidential administration of Andrew Jackson until the turn of the twentieth century, the principle of 'to the victors belong the spoils,' guided the selection of American diplomatic appointments, and our embassies and consulates abroad were staffed by political appointees.

The Consular Service was reformed in 1906, with entry examinations required, followed soon after by the Diplomatic Service (except ambassadors, who continued to be politically appointed from among cronies of the party in power). The Diplomatic and Consular Services were combined into a single Foreign Service in 1924, and the practice began of appointing some ambassadors from its ranks. With the United States attaining super power status after World War II and the proliferation of independent countries as European countries granted independence to their overseas colonies, more and more ambassadors were chosen from the ranks of career Foreign Service Officers and missions were staffed by officers and specialists from the career service.

Unlike their counterparts in the military services, however, who are often portrayed positively in popular media (movies, TV, and written literature), the Foreign Service is often distorted, ignored, or shown in a less than flattering light. Diplomats are portrayed as nitpicking bureaucrats, more concerned with the feelings of their foreign hosts than visiting Americans, or anxious to get to the next social engagement on the one hand, or devious spies plotting to do dastardly things on the other. Seldom in a movie or TV show is a diplomat shown just doing his or her job, as you see with cops and military personnel – and in *very, very few* are they shown as brave, patriotic people who are looking out for the interests of their country and its people.

In the nonfiction category, especially books written about American diplomacy, it is the top dog, or ambassador, who is often the center of attention. Seldom will the contributions of other embassy or consulate staff be mentioned. The officers, specialists, and local employees (formerly known as Foreign Service Nationals or FSNs, and now called Locally Employed Staff, or LES) are unnamed and unnoticed.

Yet, these individuals work and live in some of the most dangerous places in the world, often without the added security provided ambassadors in such environments. One has but to look at the names on the American Foreign Service Association (AFSA) Memorial Plaque in the C Street Lobby of the Department of State Building in Washington, DC, which honors members of the six American foreign affairs agencies who die while serving abroad or under conditions distinctive to overseas service. Currently, there are over 200 names inscribed, and in the dangerous world we now inhabit, with American diplomats serving in every corner, there are likely to be more.

Diplomacy, contrary to the popular media's images, is a dangerous business, and has always been.

One of America's first diplomats to make the supreme sacrifice was William Palfrey, a native of

Boston, Massachusetts, who served as an aide-de-camp to George Washington during the Revolutionary War. In November 1780, Palfrey was appointed consul general in France by Congress. He left Boston by ship and was never heard from again after the ship had left the capes.

Serving in countries where health care is limited, American diplomats have also succumbed to a variety of tropical diseases such as yellow fever and cholera, been killed in earthquakes, or by vicious mobs, and increasingly in the twentieth and twenty-first century, been the victims of terrorist attacks. There is also an unfortunately long history of attacks against American diplomatic facilities, beginning in 1900 with the Boxer Rebellion in China, when peasants in northern China, toward the end of the Qing dynasty, formed the Militia United in Righteousness (*Yihetuan)*, known in English as the 'Boxers,' which opposed foreign imperialism and Christian missionary activity. On June 21, 1900, after the Dowager Empress threw her support behind the Boxers and declared war on foreign powers, the Boxers began a 55-day siege of the foreign Legation Quarter in Peiking (now Beijing).

For a full listing of American diplomats who have lost their lives in the line of duty since 1780, see Appendix 2.

The plaque honors those who have made the ultimate sacrifice. It does not address those who face danger on a routine basis in carrying out their duties and who survive the encounters. Whether it's braving the threat of roadside bombs in Afghanistan, dealing with overly aggressive security forces in Vietnam, or working in Ebola-stricken countries of West Africa, the men and women of America's diplomatic service go where they're needed, and serve quietly and with honor.

This book, as brief as it is, is intended to honor all

who serve, who have served, and who will serve in the future, in places most Americans have never heard of, advancing and protecting our national interests, protecting and aiding Americans in distress, and promoting American industry. They're unheralded, often known but to their families and immediate colleagues, and they don't often make the evening news. But, we can be thankful that, despite the lack of acknowledgment, they continue to volunteer to go into the trenches.

There are too many to name them all. The brief essays contained herein, however, represent them and what they do. Shown here are the dangers and frustrations they face on a daily basis.

Stories from the trenches

In their own words

Americans who have served the country abroad as diplomats share their stories. While only a few are represented here, they cover a broad spectrum – Foreign Service and Civil Service, career diplomat and political appointee, and first-tour junior officer to ambassador.

A JUNIOR OFFICER HAS TO STEP UP TO THE PLATE

Gene Marshall *was a junior officer on his first posting in Damascus, Syria in 1966 when a faction of the Bath Arab Socialist Party staged a takeover of the Syrian government. He served in Damascus from 1965 to 1967.*

My first post was Embassy Damascus, Syria. The Syrians were ambivalent about our presence; they wanted contact with the US on their terms but also saw us as a stalking horse for their arch enemy, Israel, as well as being an enemy in our own right. In the police state that was Syria, this limited the possibilities for developing personal contacts and the conduct of any routine business from which the Syrian Government did not realize a great benefit. The antagonistic official atmosphere weighed heavily, but, thank goodness, routine individual contacts, such as shopping, tourism, and travel, rarely reflected the official suspicion. For a first-tour junior officer, however, this situation produced a veritable catalog of extreme diplomatic learning experiences.

In February 1966 one faction of the Baath Arab Socialist Party carried out a coup d'état, the bloodiest up to that point, against their ruling colleagues. At the time, I lived diagonally across the street from the Mohajerine Palace (used only ceremonially by the president) in a seventh floor apartment (only a three floor walk-up from the entrance on the up-hill side) surrounded by a wide terrace. When the shooting started at the palace just before dawn, I calculated possible trajectories, rolled off my bed into the corner, and went back to sleep until the Ambassador's telephone call with warnings and instructions for the embassy staff.

Six years later, shortly after I arrived in Kabul, Afghanistan, Mohammad Daoud mounted a coup against his relative, King Zahir Shah. Not yet in permanent quarters, I was house sitting two short blocks behind the radio station, which was one of the targets of the coup -- so I did a replay of Damascus 1966.

Later, there was a counter-coup in Damascus which failed. The only repercussions affecting us were a couple days of curfew, a couple weeks of travel restrictions, and the effort to find out how things were playing out in the absence of any overt sources of information.

Mid-way through my tour in Damascus our Embassy received our first defector - from the Chinese Embassy. In support of their Chinese friends, the Syrian Government would not allow him to leave, so he had to stay in the Embassy until clandestine arrangements could be made. In addition to "casserole duty" by all the wives, everyone was warned to stay away from the curbs when out walking, especially if there was a vehicle from the Chinese Embassy on the street. It was feared that the Chinese might snatch an American hostage to exchange for their man.

At 7:00 p.m. on the evening of the first day of the 1967 Six Day War, Radio Damascus' English Language News picked up Nasser's charge that the U. S. had provided air cover for the Israeli "preemptive" attacks on Cairo and Damascus. The following day, acting on instructions, the Ambassador demanded an immediate meeting with the Foreign Minister to refute these charges and protest their airing. When he arrived at the Ministry that evening, expecting to meet the Foreign Minister, he was received by a low level functionary who, reading from notes, declared a break in diplomatic relations with the U. S. and gave our staff 48 hours to leave the country. The Ambassador called everyone to the Embassy and gave us the word. We immediately began to destroy documents, something we had not been permitted to start doing earlier. As the work continued the following afternoon, just after the USIS driver, contrary to instructions, had parked the USIS station wagon in front of the Embassy gate, a mob appeared, shouting "down with America" and torched the vehicle. The Marine Guards managed to bar the front doors just in time so that, even after breaking the door glass and starting another fire, the wrought iron tracery held and the demonstrators were not able to enter the building. At this point several of us working in the secure area had gone to the roof and stood looking down on the fire at the front door. Perhaps inspired by a recent visit to the Krak des Chevaliers (best-preserved crusader castle in the Near East), someone said, "Ooh, for a pot of boiling oil." Security forces arrived quickly at that point and the demonstrators were disbursed. One officer commented that, with the timely arrival of security, the Syrian Government's orchestration was better than usual.

The U. S. Consulate in Aleppo was not so fortunate.

On the third day of the Six Day War, a friendly embassy alerted us that their consulate in Aleppo had just reported the U. S. Consulate had been sacked and burned. The Embassy's access to long distance phone lines had been cut, but the Embassy still had local service, while our home phones still retained full service. A senior embassy officer went home to attempt to phone Aleppo and canvass around for additional information - especially the status of our staff there, while a middle grade officer went to our informants in hopes they either had more information or could get through again to their consulate. Both officers then called their gleanings in to me at the Embassy, using local lines, and I took notes. With time of the essence, I entered the "holy of holies" (code room) where, lacking clearance, I had rather pointedly not been permitted entrance only days before, and dictated the first notice of the attack to the Department of State -- directly to the code clerk from my hand-written notes. No hard copy of the message ever existed in the Embassy; neither the Ambassador nor any other senior officer authorized the message, and it was unusual, to say the least, for a junior officer to send a message with the highest order of precedence - Flash.

OUT OF THE FRYING PAN, INTO THE FIRE

Jim Maher was an active duty Foreign Service Officer from 1990 to 2010. He served in Mogadishu, Somalia from November 1990 to January 1991, a brief assignment that was interrupted by the need to evacuate the embassy and all noncombatants from that war-torn country.

During my time in the Foreign Service, 1990-2010, I served in Somalia, Bosnia, Kuwait, with a period of temporary duty (TDY) Baghdad. I also had the 'pleasure' of living in terrorist areas in Greece and Peru, as well as South Korea during the transition of Kim Jong Il and family in communist North Korea.

My most memorable assignment, though, was a brief posting to Embassy Mogadishu from November 1990 through January 1991. Prior to my arrival with my family we were warned that the situation could become tense, or even chaotic. An understatement, since the Ambassador and his family were robbed at gunpoint just prior to our arrival.

By early December 1990, the situation had deteriorated, and plans were made to evacuate non-essential personnel. My recall of specific dates is a bit hazy, but I believe that the departures began around December 10; the ordered departure commenced on December 12.

The departures were a fiasco for State personnel. Kenya Air was to bring in a large plane, but only a small one arrived. One flight from Air Somalia was unable to restart its engines; the ground power unit had been stripped of its batteries, and was useless. Our innovative facilities manager and several of the others tried to jump start the GPU by hooking up our vehicles to it. That failed. A propeller plane under contract to the UN tried to back up to the jet, and use the prop wash to spin the turbines; another failure. Ultimately there were three failed attempts to evacuate our families before we achieved success with the fourth plane.

After each attempt to evacuate, families had to return to the Embassy, since there was only minimal security at the airport. While awaiting flights at the airport, the Marines kept our children safe in LAVs, feeding them and keeping their minds on things other than the deteriorating security in the area.

Meanwhile, back at the Embassy, our Regional Security Officer (RSO) was absent on his scheduled rest and recuperation travel (R&R), so we had a TDY RSO from Abidjan in charge of security. Our local guard force was managed by a former British SAS Sergeant-Major, and he took over much of the actual physical aspects of our security. He did a fantastic job.

For the next several weeks the situation grew more perilous, with numerous rounds hitting the Embassy grounds and buildings. These were mainly from small arms, usually randomly fired, but occasionally aimed. Our only respite came during the daily calls to prayer by our Somali Muslims.

Things continued to go downhill, but our Ambassador kept in contact with Washington, via Embassy Nairobi. Washington looked at a number of options for getting us out, including air dropping part of the 82nd Airborne, using the French Foreign Legion from Djibouti, etc. We, on the other hand, were down to 38 Americans at the Embassy, and were considering driving overland to Kenya as a last resort.

Finally General Schwarzkopf authorized the use of the USS Guam, a helicopter carrier, and the USS Trenton, a cruiscr providing security escort; the two vessels were diverted from the Persian Gulf, where they were preparing for the launching of Operation Desert Storm.

In the days until we were evacuated our local guard force heroically kept our compound secure, and with the assistance of our RSO and others helped to evacuate 10 other Embassies and bring their staffs into our compound. At the same time our Ambassador allowed a number of our FSNs to take refuge in our compound, at the school. No one could remember where the keys were to the doors, so I enjoyed breaking a couple windows to gain entry. This "vandalism" was a childhood dream come true.

One of the USAID employees who remained with us took over the Embassy's snack bar, and fed approximately 400 people two meals each day for over a week, using whatever she could find. Our main course was usually pasta, but at least it was food.

The night before our evacuation a number of Somalis tried to come over the walls, but were denied entry. It was messy. Our Ambassador ordered no lethal force except under threat of bodily harm, but....

On January 5, 1991, around 6 in the morning I received a call from our deputy chief of mission (DCM), telling me to go outside and see what was happening. I was in our administrative building, several hundred yards from the main chancery. I got out just in time to see 2 Navy CH-53 helicopters arrive, with a force of 60 Marines. It was like watching a John Wayne movie. The Helicopters were accompanied by an AC-130 gunship. The city immediately fell silent.

At the time the Marines arrived, and unknown to him, our Marine gunnery sergeant was single-handedly denying entry at the back gate of the compound. He stood up to a truck load of armed Somalis who were trying to get in. He was subsequently awarded the Bronze Star for valor for this act of bravery. At the last minute all the Somalis inexplicably backed off, got in their truck and fled in reverse. Our Marine was mystified until he turned around and saw a squad of the arriving Marines had taken up firing positions behind him.

Apart from the CH-53s, a number of smaller Helos began arriving, airlifting 285 of us, including the other Embassies' staffs, to the Guam and the Trenton. The after action reports indicated that we probably got out within an hour of the Embassy being overrun.

RAGING MOBS AND SPIDER BITES

Jon Dorschner *describes the chaos in Dhaka, Bangladesh after the start of the first Gulf War, and dealing with the backlash from Iraqi sympathizers.*

From 1990-1992, I was assigned to the Political Section of the US Embassy in Dhaka, Bangladesh. This was during the first Gulf War. Bangladesh was one of the first Islamic countries to commit troops to the anti-Iraq alliance. The Iraqi Embassy immediately vowed revenge and organized an attack on the American Club, the American Embassy, the British Embassy and the Saudi Embassy. My house was immediately behind the American club. We heard a fleet of trucks pull up in front of the club. We went to our rooftop to see what was happening. Hundreds of bearded madrasah students emerged from the trucks and with much shouting scaled the walls surrounding the club. They went from room to room destroying as much as they could and stealing whatever they could get their hands on. The American and Bangladeshi staff had already fled the building. There was no sign of Bangladeshi security.

Suddenly, Bangladeshi Army trucks arrived and disgorged elite troops. The attackers began to flee the building in panic carrying whatever they could steal, including napkins, silverware, and tablecloths. The Bangladeshi troops chased them and beat those they caught with their rifles. Within minutes, the attack was over the participants had fled in all directions.

I then went to the Embassy. The Marines were installing concertina wire above the gates of the building, which was built like a medieval fortress with very few entry points. The Marines stood at the entry points cradling their shotguns and awaiting the attack. After attacking the American club, the mob had reconstituted and attacked the British and Saudi Embassies, breaking windows and causing destruction. They then moved on to the American Embassy and congregated outside. There was no way for them to get inside however, and no outside windows that they could break or use to gain entry. They did not want to confront the Marines or get entangled in the concertina wire. With no alternative, they began to chant anti-American slogans and took off their shoes and waved the bottoms at the Embassy. While this is considered a great insult in South Asia, it meant nothing to the Marines who found it quite funny. The mob then pelted the Embassy with rocks, which bounced off of the brick face of the building and broke the few exterior lights.

We endured the rain of rocks for several minutes until the Bangladesh Army arrived and again dispersed the mob. That night, the commander of the Army forces blockaded the bridges leading into the diplomatic enclave. He let it be known that any attempt to cross the bridges would be met by overwhelming military force. He set up machine guns in sandbag emplacements to cover the approaches. In addition, he built sandbag emplacements throughout the enclave, which were manned by troops with automatic weapons.

That night, the Ambassador announced that all family members and "non-essential" personnel would be evacuated. My family left the following morning. I was alone in the house with the servants for the next three months. We were confined to the diplomatic enclave. I rode to work every day in an armored vehicle accompanied by Bangladeshi troops. I worked out an escape plan with the servants should the house come under attack. We placed ladders in key locations so that we could scale the wall and escape. I arranged with my Bangladeshi neighbors to provide me with safe haven and slip me out of the area should my house come under attack.

During this period I was active in working with the Bangladeshi government to curtail the ability of the Iraqi Embassy to sponsor more attacks. The government impounded Iraqi funds and cut off Embassy communications and the Embassy quickly ran out of money. Iraqi staffers were forced to sell Embassy furniture and the building quickly became empty. The Iraqi Embassy printed thousands of leaflets with my name and address telling "good Muslims" to kill me on sight. They left the leaflets in busses and other public places. But it was apparent that Iraq had no public support.

On one occasion I was locked out of my car in the bazaar. A crowd quickly gathered. One Bangladeshi hesitantly shouted "death to America!!" and for a second, it looked like I would be attacked by an angry mob. The tension quickly deflated, however, and I was able to open my car and drive away without incident.

The strong posture of the Bangladeshi government and Army prevented the Iraqis from sponsoring further attacks. For several weeks, the demonstrators gathered in front of the entrances to the diplomatic enclave hoping to get inside and cause further mayhem, but none dared challenge the resolve of the Army commander who made it clear he would fire if any of them crossed his self-declared redline. When it became apparent that Iraq would suffer a crushing defeat, the demonstrations ceased.

As was the case in Pakistan, driving was our most dangerous activity. This was compounded by the fact that there was a long-term "uprising" against the military regime of Hussain Mohammad Ershad. This meant that in addition to the usual chaos on the streets, we had to contend with daily demonstrations and work stoppages. We continued to drive our American car with the steering wheel on the wrong side. Dhaka was home to tens of thousands of human powered bicycle rickshaws and enormous congestion, with most of the people on foot. This made driving very difficult and slow. We had to be very careful to avoid hitting and killing anyone on the street.

Disease was also a big problem. Any cut or abrasion could quickly become infected. Local medical care was completely unreliable. A colleague scraped his finger and went to a local doctor for treatment. The conditions were so unsanitary that his hand quickly became infected and he had to be evacuated to Singapore for surgery. His finger was amputated.

After a poisonous spider bit me, my foot turned bright blue. The blue color spread from my foot to my leg. The Embassy doctor drew a line half way up my leg and prescribed massive doses of antibiotics. If the blue reaches the line, he said, you will have to be evacuated, for it will be life threatening. I remained in bed in my room for days, but the blue finally receded.

THE BURNING OF CAIRO

Frances McStay Adams *was a Foreign Service spouse who served in Cairo as an assistant and the director of the Fulbright Program from 1950 to 1952 when her husband was stationed at the Embassy.*

I was in charge of the Fulbright Program in Cairo in 1950 after the person in charge had left. This was when King Farouk was still ruler of Egypt.

We were there for the burning of Cairo and when members of the Muslim Brotherhood were marching in the streets. I was walking with my son one day to a Fulbrighter's house when we saw a mob approaching. They were after foreigners, and were crossing out any words on signs that weren't in Arabic. My son and I hid behind an apartment, and fortunately they didn't find us.

It was a very dangerous time. We would have parties in our place for our friends, including Egyptians. We had a Mozart party when they were burning Cairo, and we were worried that people wouldn't come because it was so dangerous in the street, but some came anyway. Afterwards, though, they were afraid to leave – some were neighbors who stayed in apartments above us in the building, and they were afraid to go up to their places – so we just stayed up all night. We were a little afraid that they might start torching the place, but they never did.

There were some evacuations from Egypt, but not like the ones later in 1967. There were a lot of evacuations later, though.

Foreign Affairs Oral History Collection, Association for Diplomatic Studies and Training, Arlington, VA, www.adst.org.

CONSULAR WORK CAN BE HAZARDOUS TO YOUR HEALTH

Mike Meszaros, a civil service employee, who works as an Attorney-Advisor in the State Department's Bureau of Consular Affairs relates experiences that show that danger lurks for American diplomats regardless of status.

My name is Mike Meszaros and I'm an Attorney Adviser with the U.S. Department of State's Bureau of Consular Affairs. However, I do have a lot of overseas experience; and a bit of it in dangerous places. I served as the Deputy Consular Chief of the U.S. Embassy Sana'a, Yemen, from 2008-2011. We were attacked three times when I was in Yemen, with the big attack in September 2008 killing 18 people. I've seen different figures as to the number killed, but 18 is what I recall. I was sheltering in place under my desk during the attack, taking attendance and telling bad jokes to keep the morale up during the attack. My overseas experience prior to Yemen includes serving as the acting head of various consular sections six times, four times in Monrovia, Liberia (1995, 1998, 2003 and

2004), Dhaka, Bangladesh (2001) and Almaty, Kazakhstan (1997). I also served a temporary assignment in the Consular Section of Embassy Baghdad (May 2005), assisted the relatives of U.S. citizens who perished in two plane crashes (Cali, Colombia, 1995 and Halifax, Nova Scotia 1998), assisted Embassy Port au Prince during a coup (1991), assisted Embassy Granada and the Grand Cayman's evacuating American citizens in the aftermath of Hurricane Ivan (where I slept under a tarp that covered the Granada post's open roof) and conducted a crisis management exercise in Somalia with former ambassador Maura Harty in 1994.

Some of my most vivid memories of danger are my time as acting consular chief in Monrovia from July 10 to September 1, 2003. This was during the height of the "Siege of Monrovia," when small arms and mortar fire were constantly landing on or near the Embassy. When the first major mortar attack came, most of us were in the recreation hall for lunch, and I'll never forget the magnificent plume of water a mortar shell created when it impacted on the ocean.

I was quickly forced to move into the public affairs officer's (PAO) vacant house, which I shared with a number of different people, some USG and some not, who were either being evacuated or coming though on temporary duty. It was a very hasty move. I was forced to wear the same clothes for almost two weeks, and electricity issues necessitated cold water showers, which had a tendency to wake one up in the morning.

This leads into my Discovery Times Channel adventure. Several of us were in the same situation, having to move quickly from the Sam & E Apartments, which were across the street from the Embassy, onto the Embassy grounds without any toiletries. After two weeks, we organized a "rescue mission" for our missing clothes/essentials. I particularly needed a belt, and I later saw film my family recorded from NBC news of me leading people to helicopters and having to hold up my pants. (I lost about 10 pounds real quick. Working 16-18 hours a day with only two meals can have that effect). We were guarded by Marines from the FAST unit, sent to augment the post. As we lined up to make the short walk between the gate and entrance to the Sam & E, several rounds cracked into the masonry above the gate, raising our apprehension level. A high-pucker factor, as they say in the military.

We made the short walk and I gathered my things without incident. A communicator named Otis and I were the first ones through. As we were waiting in the foyer of the Sam & E, an expended AK-47 round apparently struck the wall of the Embassy, then ricocheted on to the metal door we were standing behind. It was hot to the touch when we picked it up. I still have it.

As we started to make our way back to the Embassy, a gentleman who was sheltering under a building close to the Sam & E asked us if we were "on a beer run." Looking back, I saw one of the military guys had picked up a case of Heineken and was taking it back to post.

The gentlemen who asked us about the beer run was a film producer, and in his film "Liberia an Uncivil War," we were depicted as having a "beer run" in the midst of the hostilities.

However, the film did show us in a generally positive light. I'll never forget the courageous performances of Ambassador John Blaney, DCM Duane Sams (who arrived near the end of the hostilities), Political Officer Dante Paradiso, a first tour officer who did a magnificent job, RSO Ted Collins, Defense Attaché (DATT) Sue Ann Sandusky and Assistant RSO (ARSO) Brad Lynch. The Facilities maintenance guy, the DATT's Operations Coordinator (OPSCO) and the Embassy nurse also did great jobs.

ALMOST CAPTURED BY THE ENEMY

James R. Bullington joined the Foreign Service in 1962. After serving in Washington as a desk officer for two years, he was assigned to Vietnam as a reporting officer in 1965.

In 1965, I was assigned to Vietnam. It came out of the blue; one day, I got the call, 'Hey, you're going to go to FSI and study Vietnamese for a while and go to Vietnam.' They assigned me to Hue as Vice Consul. I'd never followed Vietnam affairs. I'd heard of it, but that's about all. The war at the time was not really a big deal like it later became. We had military advisors there, but we didn't have any American combat units. Vietnam was still seen as pretty remote, and our involvement was only at the margins, or so it seemed. But, it was obviously a growing concern, and growing very quickly. The State Department was rapidly building up the embassy and what was called the Provincial Reporting Unit, which I was to be a part of even though I was stationed in Hue. It was a unit within the political section.

My job was to travel around the five provinces of I Corps, the five northernmost provinces of South Vietnam. I was to send reports to the embassy on the political and economic situations, on pacification in the countryside – those sorts of things. At FSI, I took eight or ten weeks of language training, so I could get by, but I wasn't really fluent in Vietnamese. It got a little better after I'd been there for a while, but I did have French, so I could use French with most Vietnamese I needed to talk to. All educated Vietnamese at that time spoke French.

I went to Vietnam in July 1965. I spent two or three weeks in Saigon, where I went around with some of the people in the Provincial Reporting Unit there; people like John Negroponte, Dick Holbrooke, David Lambert, and others. I observed that the situation on the ground was deteriorating. The Provincial Reporting Unit was the part of the Mission that would bring the bad news – more than any other. The MACV military chain of command was not giving as realistic reports as the embassy provincial reporters, or the journalists. This was the time when the journalists were beginning to change from supportive to more and more questioning, and sometimes downright hostile.

When I finally went to Hue, I wasn't given any special orders; just to report on the normal things you'd look for – how is the government doing, what do people think, is there corruption, is the government winning or losing, are the hamlets safe or not safe?

We had a small consulate in Hue. Sam Thomsen was the consul and I was vice consul. There were the two of us plus the communicator, Joe O'Neal, who later went to become a Foreign Service Officer, along with three or four FSN support people.

I traveled around a lot, interacting with the U.S.

advisors (mostly army officers) or staying at the Special Forces camps. I was 24, 25 at the time, and when you're that age you're invulnerable. You don't worry about danger. It was foolhardy, but I never felt a great sense of fear as I was traveling around. I did get shot at a couple of time, but as with most young people, personal safety wasn't at the top of my concern. It should have been.

Things were becoming tense in Hue. One day I was to deliver a message to Thich Tri Quang the leader of the Buddhists, and just as I was finishing doing that, a firefight broke out between Vietnamese troops around the pagoda and the Catholics in the neighboring area. My interpreter and I managed to get back to the consulate. The situation continued to worsen, becoming increasingly anti-American, with daily demonstrations outside the consulate. Finally, in March 1966, student demonstrators burned the consulate and the USIA library.

After the consulate was burned, I was assigned to the embassy in Saigon as staff aide to Henry Cabot Lodge.

In 1967, I was in Quang Tri, the northernmost province, right on the DMZ. That's where we had the big war, with large combat units and some big, big battles. My job there was to take care of the refugees and help resettle them to the south in a place called Cam Lo. While this was going on, there were major invasions by the North Vietnamese.

I decided to visit Hue on January 30, 1968, which proved to be a poor choice of timing, as this was when the Tet Offensive started. That night, I was awakened by the sounds of incoming mortars. It was evident that some serious fighting was going on. Previously, attacks by the North Vietnamese or Viet Cong on major towns had been hit and run affairs, so by dawn when things had quieted down, I thought it was over. When I emerged from the guest house where I was staying, I saw armed men wearing pith helmets at the end of the courtyard who obviously weren't friendlies. The NVA had set up a command post right there where I was staying.

With the help of a French friend, I was able to get out of the guest house and to a house of two French priests. There was pretty intense fighting, especially when friendly forces counterattacked. The two-story French Colonial house we were in took a direct hit from 105 mm artillery shell, becoming one-story all of a sudden. We were huddled downstairs under the staircase and were unhurt.

After nine days, the U.S. Marines, working their way house to house in fierce combat throughout Hue, got to where I was and liberated me. The company commander was Ron Christmas, who later became a Marine lieutenant general. I was never so glad to see anyone as Captain Christmas and his Marines. They wrapped me in a blanket and carried me out as if I were a wounded Marine, so the neighbors would not see that these priests had been harboring an American. I had invited, in fact urged, the two priests to come with me to safety, but they had pastoral duties they felt kept them there.

The Marines took me to MACV headquarters. I spent one night there, and was interviewed by reporters. The next day, the story of my liberation was on the front page of the *Washington Post*. In fact, that' show my parents found out about it – through a newspaper report. They'd been told by the State Department that I was missing.

Foreign Affairs Oral History Collection, Association for Diplomatic Studies and Training, Arlington, VA, www.adst.org.

WHAT'S NORMAL ANYWAY?

Frank Lavin served as U.S. Ambassador to the Republic of Singapore, 2001-2005 when he departed to assume the position of U.S. Undersecretary of Commerce. He previously served in the Reagan and Bush (41) Administrations. He currently serves as CEO of Export Now, helping U.S. companies enter the China market.

America was transported to a 3 a.m. moment just a few months ago when we learned of the assault on our Benghazi Consulate and the murder of Chris Stephens and the other Americans who worked there. I never had the honor of knowing Ambassador Stephens, but I knew in an instant what happened. A version of the Benghazi assault almost unfolded in Singapore some ten years previously. Indeed reading of the murders in Libya, I had an acute wave of nausea, so sharp I had to call my wife to walk through the episode. This earlier event had implications for policy, counter-terrorism, and embassy management, as well as a human dimension. Let me take you back...

I first heard of the 3 a.m. moment in 2001 while participating in the required two-week training on Embassy leadership as I was going through the nomination process to serve as the U.S. Ambassador to Singapore. One of the exercises included something of a trick question: What is the most important article of clothing for an ambassador? Is it white tails, for state weddings and funerals? Is it black tails, for formal dances and banquets? Is it an ordinary business suit for ministry calls?   Other ideas were also put forward, but the reason this was a trick question is that the answer was – pajamas and a bathrobe. Because the success of your mission will not necessarily be determined by the normal course of business or state occasions, but by the emergency that unfolds at the wrong time. And you will find yourself in crisis management with your country team at 3 a.m. in the Ambassador's Residence. Better get some good PJs and a respectable robe.

After the September 11 attacks, the United States and allies went into Afghanistan to defeat al-Qaeda (AQ). A majority of the U.S. forces that went into Afghanistan came through Singapore, including all forces from Hawaii, Guam, Japan and the west coast of the United States. It is not clear if this fact was known by AQ or to what extent it affected their planning, but we do know that as a response to the Allied invasion of Afghanistan, AQ decided to inflict a massive attack in Singapore. This was to be their first strike post-9/11.

I arrived at post in August 2001 to begin duties, but I only entered this narrative in early December, when I was alerted by the Singapore Government that the U.S. embassy had been targeted by AQ and their affiliate Jemaah Islamiyah (JI) to be destroyed by a car bomb. Our embassy was briefed by the Singapore

Internal Security Department (ISD) that the ammonia nitrate to make the bomb had been procured, as had fuses and a truck. So the plot was perhaps days away from being operational. The local terrorist cell had done all the work, and the suicide drivers were to be "imported" for the final step.

This news was immediately confirmed by British special forces in Afghanistan who had uncovered a videotape in an AQ safe house - a surveillance tape of our embassy with a discussion of how to kill us.

I had the opportunity to review the video tape and it contained the same chilling mixture of amateurishness and lethality shown by the 9/11 terrorists. The tapes had light-hearted banter, a discussion of security barriers, and a plan to kill. The attack was to be a two-step, with the first truck bomb to detonate against our security gates allowing the second and larger truck bomb to drive through and destroy our embassy. By December, the terrorists had amassed four tons of ammonia nitrate.

The British High Commission, the Australian High Commission, U.S. Naval facilities, Singapore businesses and the Israeli Embassy were also targeted. I remembered from training that this two-bomb approach was how AQ attacked the U.S. Embassies in Kenya and Tanzania in 1998. What was instructive about that incident was that the first bomb drew people to the windows, which allowed the second bomb to kill them with flying shards of window glass. This attack resulted in the deaths of over 200 people and also resulted in the FBI adding a new name to their list of top ten fugitives – Osama bin Laden.

Just three years later, bin Laden was now targeting another U.S. embassy. We were told by the ISD that while the killers were preparing to get us, Singapore was preparing to get them.

We were to be the cheese in the mousetrap, under

orders to "act normal." We could not leave post, change our routine, or let word slip out lest we warn the terrorists that we were on to their game. Importantly, we could not even notify the entire embassy, due to the "no double standard" rule. This rule, imposed after the Pan Am 103 bombing meant that any terrorist threat shared within the U.S. Government community also had also to be shared with the general American community, an entirely reasonable requirement. So to avoid a violation of that rule, we could only discuss the threat with the security team responsible for countering it.

We undertook our plans, the terrorists undertook their plans, and the ISD also had plans. The ISD focused on technical and physical surveillance of the terrorists to make sure they had uncovered the entire cell, the leadership, their payment methods, the parties with whom they were communicating, and so forth. Any pre-mature disruption of the plot would also disrupt the intelligence work. So we had to go along.

On one level, our plans simply required a certain discipline to go through daily routines knowing that murderers were watching and waiting. I took solace in knowing that our troops in the field were facing far greater danger. As the U.S., U.K., and Australian diplomatic facilities were adjoining, this allowed for regular communication and a minute by minute feel among the three missions. Citizens of Britain, Australia, and Israel should take pride that their countries send diplomats of the caliber of Alan Collins, Gary Quinlan, and Itzak Shoham who served with resolve and steadiness during this time.

On another level, there were steps we could take to prepare us for when the truck bomb came. We were able to review perimeter security architecture, blast standards, rules of engagement, fire and control mechanism and so forth. I went to the shooting range with our Marine detachment to make sure my pistol qualifications were current. More important, I wanted to spend time with the Marines, to make sure they could recognize my voice when the power was down, the back-up systems were down, and the room was full of smoke.

We made sure we had the special equipment – we each had individual breathing apparatus to get us through smoke inhalation or a white powder incident. We had individual auto-injectors with atropine which was supposed to protect against nerve agents. However, it was never properly explained how we were to determine if a nerve agent was being used.

Secure communications links with Washington remained intact and we had a number of consultations with the State Department during this period. State deserves high marks for responsiveness and thoroughness. All parties concluded there was really nothing more that could be done. We believed we had forces adequate to our mission. It didn't come down to extra resources. It came down to reliance on our Singaporean hosts to disrupt the plot, reliance on our own backbone to play our role, and reliance in the final instance on our own firepower to halt a truck bomb sufficiently far from our gates so as to save the lives in the embassy.

And what does it mean to "act normal?" How long does it take to shave in the morning? How long do you spend at the gym – or should one be at the gym at all? It evoked T.S. Eliot –"I have measured out my life in coffee spoons" - as we had to measure out our days in precise increments to ensure we were staying true to form. Sometimes I was more inspired by Eric Idle and greeted the new day with a jaunty "I'm not dead yet."

A person was observed sketching the house of the Defense Minister. It turned out she was an innocent architectural student completing a homework assignment.

Separately, our counter-surveillance detail noticed a person who would appear at the bus stop across the street from the embassy at approximately the same time every day, but who never seemed to board a bus. He would loiter at the stop for a few minutes and then walk off the way he came. We notified the police but when they arrived he had already disappeared. This behavior repeated itself daily, at roughly the same time, and for several days in a row the pedestrian managed to elude the authorities. When they managed to nab him, he turned out to be an ordinary citizen who was under doctor's order to walk one km a day, and our bus stop was exactly ½ km from his apartment.

This bit of cat and mouse went on for about ten days when to our enormous relief, the trap was spring. The ISD arrested 15 terrorists and the following August an additional 21 were picked up. Singapore deserves high praise for its professionalism in rolling up the terrorist cell. In fighting terrorism, we are either going to be a minute early or a minute late, and I was glad that in this case we were a minute early.

Bali

The good news in Singapore soon turned into bad news some months later in Bali. Indeed JI stated that they concluded that Singapore was a hard target and they needed to find a soft target. This all but guaranteed we would be a minute late.

Last Oct 12, we observed the 10th anniversary of the Bali Blast. 202 people murdered by terrorists, among them 7 Americans. The Bali attack joined the Kenya/Tanzania attacks as two of only a dozen terrorist attacks that killed over 200 people.

I dispatched our embassy's two FBI agents to Bali to assist the Indonesian investigators. The Australian Federal Police and Scotland Yard also sent help. The FBI had the unpleasant job of visiting the hotel rooms to which no one had returned to retrieve genetic material from the toothbrushes. That allowed forensic specialists to establish a DNA match against the burned corpses recovered from the bombing.

More profitably, they then had the assignment of identifying all properties leased on Bali in the previous six months that could accommodate a vehicle and had an enclosed garage, this after having determined that the bomb was likely assembled on the island and not brought in on a ferry. It was this bit of patient detective work that led to discovery of the bomb assembly site and provided the clues that led to the first wave of arrests.

We took the American victims to burn units in Singapore and I had the chance to visit with them in the hospital and to make sure we connected with their families in the U.S.

I asked Australian High Commissioner Gary Quinlan what we could to help the more numerous Australian victims and he said that there was an urgent need for donated blood. We posted a flash request to the American community in Singapore and by the end of the day the Singapore Red Cross asked us to stop because they had no more capacity; the response had overwhelmed their systems.

So the pattern we saw in Libya unfolded in Singapore via Bali: we help the wounded; we mourn the dead; we cherish our loved ones; we grow and (we hope) we learn. We fight back.

Ten years after these episodes, what are the lessons? First, close coordination with the host government is an essential security requirement. Even the best protected diplomatic facility is not designed to defend against a sustained assault. Core responsibility for security must be assumed by the host country. In our case, the Government of Singapore deserves high praise for professionalism and responsiveness. The silver lining in this somewhat bleak situation was that the Government of Singapore took its duties seriously, and had the people and the systems to make the difference. Notably, the Malaysian and Indonesian security services also did good work in breaking up JI operations in their countries as well.

Second, good intelligence is an essential security requirement. Our ability to get raw intelligence from the British and from the ISD as well as our internal capabilities helped us predict what AQ would do and to devise mechanisms to counter.

Third, don't confuse popularity with security. Maintain a preponderance of force. One of the more poignant elements of the Chris Stephens murder were the comments as to how popular he was in Libya, how he had worked with the insurgent groups in the overthrow of Khadafy and how the ordinary Libyans had warm feelings toward him. This fact is important, but not directly related to his security. Indirectly it probably undermined his security because it made him a target. Any U.S. Ambassador might be a trophy target. You need to be a hard target as well.

Fourth, work with what you have. The U.S. Government has enormous resources and capabilities, but access to these strengths are constrained by bureaucracy and war-time exigencies. On one hand, our ability to command additional resources and to get them on station was severely limited. On the other hand, we did not believe we needed additional resources. One of our embassy people commented with gallows humor that the U.S. Government will spend more money on your funeral than it will on your protection. I do not think that this statement is literally true, but it does highlight that the U.S. Government tends to act the most rapidly after a crisis has occurred.

Fifth, management, training, morale, and communications all matter. An Ambassador should have entrance interviews with every new embassy personnel for a reason. You want to establish a pattern of communication and responsibility from the start. An Ambassador should attend the Marine's Friday bar-b-q for a reason. That's your town hall meeting, when any member of the embassy community can approach you on any topic. I was at the pistol range not because I believed it likely that I would be firing rounds at the terrorists, but also because it was an effective way of communicating with the Marines and showing leadership. For management integrity, I had to ensure I was at the embassy every single day during this threat – the entire day – visible and upbeat with the entire security team.

We reviewed all of our security procedures and went through training with our security team to review contingencies. Fortunately we had a modern embassy structure and grounds, a "Class A" facility in the jargon. We had useful discussions with technical support at State to review gate specifics and blast standards. We knew the importance of "set-backs" and blast perimeters: The 1996 Khobar Tower bombing in Saudi Arabia killed 19 U.S. Airmen with a bomb detonated *outside* the security fence.

I made it a point to signal to the general public that we were prepared to use force, but to do so in a low-key fashion – we love having visitors, but please call ahead. If your Frisbee inadvertently comes into our yard, please do not hop the fence to retrieve it.

Six, terrorism cannot be defeated only by foiling attacks. To borrow from the Hymn, it is not enough to unleash a swift sword; you have to also trample out the vineyards where the grapes of wrath are stored. This is a topic beyond this essay, but we can make a few observations. Not only is the United States a different nation than ten years ago but Indonesia is as well. The U.S. has worked closely with Indonesia to help that country strengthen its democratic structures, keep economic growth on track, and build a counter-terrorist capability. Indonesia's journey is far from complete but the work of the U.S., Australia, and others over the past decade has helped it considerably.

Finally, in counter-terrorism you will likely either be a minute early or a minute late. In the cases of Kenya, Tanzania, Libya, and Bali – support was a minute late. I am grateful that in my case we were a minute ahead of the enemy.

An American friend said when it was all over – you were just in the wrong place at the wrong time. My feeling was just the opposite - I was in the right place at the right time. I don't mind a 3 a.m. call. I had the chance to provide leadership, to see the mission through, to help defeat a terrorist cell, and to strengthen our ties with a good friend in the process. Perhaps the most notable element of this story is that this is not unusual for U.S. diplomats. It's what Ambassadors are supposed to do.

FAMILY MEMBERS SHARE THE RISKS

Colonel (retired) Dave Jesmer *served as a Defense Attaché in Damascus, Syria and Amman, Jordan. .*

My family also experienced a terrorist attack in Damascus in April 2004. A carload of Islamic militants were stopped on the street in front of my house (the Beirut-Damascus Highway), and then drove across the street and occupied a home, forcing the elderly couple who lived there out the back. This house was 5 homes from my house on the same street. A firefight ensued between various Syrian security forces and the terrorists, and included RPGs, machineguns and grenades. After an hour, all of the terrorists were either dead or wounded and captured (though the detainees eventually died while "escaping"). A female school principle across the street was killed, as was the Syrian guard at the British Ambassador's residence behind my home and several passersby. I was home at the time and placed my family in an interior closet while I maintained communications with the embassy and Washington, and dashed across the street behind my house to check on the family of my assistant army attaché (he was on a mission along the border between Iraq and Syria at the time). When the fighting died down, I went out to investigate and sent in reports. We found bullets and shrapnel around our home. My sons still write about this firefight in various essays and school assignments.

During an earlier assignment in Amman, Jordan we experienced the spillover effects of the second intifada--demonstrations at the embassy, etc. We were at the beach in Aqaba when I was called back to destroy classified holdings. We were later locked down in our homes as the embassy was closed due to the demonstrations and threats. Perhaps your readers would be interested in learning about the 'safe haven' that was built into our house and many others. Our second floor master bedroom was equipped with a hardened steel door and bars on the windows. We stored extra water and military meals (MREs) in the closet, along with a rope ladder. We had our embassy radio in this room.

A week or so later, USAID friends of ours were driving on a Friday afternoon following the afternoon prayers from the citadel in downtown Amman back to the embassy when they drove into the back of a demonstration heading to the embassy. The demonstrators turned around and started stoning and attacking the car. Family members suffered minor injuries (though the father was hospitalized briefly) and they departed the country in the following month.

For what it's worth, I was in Beirut at the time of the first embassy bombing as well (April 1983). I was part of a Special Forces (SF) training team living in a bayside hotel about 400 meters down the *corniche* from the old embassy. We typically sent back a few folks from my training site at the airport to the embassy for our mail and lunch, but that particular day we were so busy starting the training program for a new Lebanese Army battalion that my team members returned to the airport rather than staying for lunch. The explosion blew in my hotel windows and the sliding door to my balcony. A few days later, members of my team acted as pallbearers at the airport to transfer the coffins of the American dead from Lebanese hearses to the waiting US Air Force aircraft for the return home. Shortly thereafter, the US Marines at the airport provided some equipment to enable our construction of a large dirt berm around the hotel (closing off the *corniche*). We then hosted many of the embassy functions at our hotel, and my SF colleagues and I provided security along with a Lebanese Army company. We were subsequently ordered to move in with the Marines at the airport "for our safety." We delayed our move for a few months insisting that bunkers be constructed next to the tents in which we were supposed to live. That plan was eventually shelved following the October suicide bombing of the Marine barracks.

WHAT A WAY TO CELEBRATE THE NEW YEAR

Charles Ray joined the U.S. Foreign Service in 1982 after serving 20 years in the U.S. Army. He served in China, Thailand, Sierra Leone, Vietnam, Cambodia, and Zimbabwe, as well as tours in the Bureau of Politico-Military Affairs, Diplomat in residence at the University of Houston, and Deputy Assistant Secretary of Defense for POW/Missing Personnel Affairs. From 2002 to 2005, he was ambassador to the Kingdom of Cambodia.

I arrived in Cambodia on December 26, 2002 to begin my assignment as ambassador. Because it was the holiday season, my work load was minimal – I spent much of my time getting to know the embassy and my staff and introducing myself to other members of the diplomatic community. Until I presented my credentials to the head of state, King Norodom Sihanouk, I could not participate in any other public activities.

I presented my credentials on January 4, 2003, in an impressive ceremony at the royal palace, and my work started in earnest.

The Cambodian elections were scheduled for later in the year, we were reviewing our support of the extensive demining programs in the country, there was increased pressure from human rights lobbyists in Washington to monitor and report on political violence and intimidation, and we had to deal with a steady stream of visitors.

With all this on my plate, I paid scant attention to a small controversy that cropped up early in January regarding a report in a Cambodian newspaper alleging that a Thai TV actress had made a comment in a TV show that 'she would never come to Cambodia until the country gave Angkor Wat back to Thailand,' or words to that effect. Other papers, TV and radio stations picked up this unsubstantiated story and it soon spread nationwide. Prime Minister Hun Sen added fuel to the fire by saying in a public speech that the actress in question 'wasn't worth a blade of grass around the temples.'

At the embassy, we noted this little brouhaha, but otherwise paid little attention to it. On January 28, we'd welcomed a visiting group from the U.S. Defense Department's office concerned with the recovery of U.S. remains from the Vietnam War. I personally accompanied them during their visits to Cambodian government officials, including the defense minister and the chief of the defense staff.

We'd just left a meeting in mid-afternoon on January 29, and were on our way back to the embassy when I noticed a large group of young people, on foot and on bikes, moving toward Norodom Boulevard, one of the city's main north-south arteries. There'd been a number of demonstrations in connection with the upcoming elections, all relatively peaceful, so I didn't pay any special attention.

Later that evening, along with the defense delegation, I attended a reception hosted by the Cambodian defense minister at the Hotel Le Royal. About an hour into the reception, the Cambodian officials began receiving calls on their cell phones and looked worried. After the defense minister received a call, I asked what was up. He hesitated, but then said that there was a demonstration taking place in front of the Thai embassy, and the police were not handling it very well. He feared the army would have to be deployed to disperse the demonstrators, and apologized that the reception would have to end.

The delegation was staying at the hotel, so that only left my defense attaché, Colonel Steve Rundle and me to get back to our residences. On the way out, however, we were able to get a bit more information about what was going on. It turned out that the group of young people I'd seen earlier in the day had been students on their way to the Thai Embassy on Norodom Boulevard to stage a protest over the reported TV broadcast. Police were called, but the protesters had stayed outside the embassy compound. As the day wore on, though, the protesters became more aggressive, and some had forced their way over the walls and into the compound, and were burning tires and smashing car windows. The police, who had done nothing to stop the protesters up to that point, reported that they were unable to establish control. The calls being received by our defense ministry hosts were reports of Molotov cocktails being thrown at the embassy building, and protesters trying to force their way inside the building, which by now had been evacuated by the staff. Police said they had lost control and were requesting army assistance.

When I arrived at my residence, some five

kilometers from the Thai embassy, I alerted Alex Arvizu, my deputy chief of mission (DCM) and directed him to assemble the emergency action committee (EAC). We sent word out to the embassy staff to remain in their residences and stay alert, and had American citizens in Phnom Penh notified through the warden network to avoid crowds and stay at home. In the meantime, working from my home office, a room overlooking Norodom Avenue, I was on three phones; my cell phone, my wife's cell phone, and the house landline; trying to keep abreast of what was going on. On one phone, I stayed in contact with the EAC which had convened at the embassy, keeping one available for calls to or from Washington if necessary. On my wife's cell, I was in contact with the wife of the Japanese ambassador. Their residence was next door to the Thai embassy, and she provided me a minute-by-minute update on what she was seeing from her bedroom window. I relayed this information to the EAC, which was the official contact with Washington and the local American community.

For over an hour, I watched as more and more protestors on motorbikes rode past my house in the direction of the Thai embassy. Around midnight, I heard what might have been gunfire, and soon saw large numbers of young people on bikes heading quickly in the opposite direction. By one in the morning, things were quiet.

I went in to the embassy the next morning, January 30, and got a briefing from the DCM. Colonel Rundle did a drive through the city and came back around noon to brief me on what he'd seen. He reported that the city was quiet, but the Thai embassy and ambassador's residence had been burned, and several Thai businesses had been sacked. Vehicular and foot traffic, amazingly enough, was moving throughout the city normally, and people were walking by and looking at the damage like tourists visiting Angkor Wat. The sense of calm was surreal. Considering the damage to property, it was also amazing that the casualty figures were so low. There was one report of a body found, but we were never able to figure out if it was connected with the riots. There were a number of arrests (most of those arrested were later acquitted and released), and we learned that the disturbances had been confined to Phnom Penh.

While the average citizens seemed calm, there was tension in government. Relations between Thailand and Cambodia are always somewhat strained, and when the riots broke out, the borders between them were closed by Thai authorities to Thai and Cambodian citizens until March 21.

Eventually, after Cambodia paid reparations for the damage to the Thai embassy, things went back to what passes for normal in their bilateral relations, and this incident became just another story to be told when diplomats who were there gather – just a routine part of our jobs.

BOMBING OF THE BEIRUT EMBASSY

Anne Dammarell *served as a USAID General Development Officer in Beirut, Lebanon from 1980 to 1984.*

In 1980, the personnel office at USAID was looking for someone to go to Lebanon and asked me if I'd go. I said yes because I'd known Lebanese as a kid and liked them. That was my *sophisticated* response. I knew there was a civil war, but didn't know exactly what that meant. I knew there was danger of a sort, but I was not prepared for the World War II images that I saw driving along the *corniche* from the airport to the embassy. The *corniche*, a coastal road right along the Mediterranean, had beautiful views of the water, but the buildings were bombed out and there were checkpoints. There must have been more than 10 militia groups, each with a different section of the city to guard.

Our living arrangements were quite good. I had a three-bedroom apartment on the *corniche*, a five-minute walk from the embassy. It was very comfortable.

The militias were like private armies. I don't have a military background, so in the beginning they all looked like military or police to me, although some didn't wear uniforms. Our vehicles had diplomatic plates, so they knew we were Americans and usually just waved us through. It was still a bottleneck, though, because if we were behind a car without diplomatic plates, we'd have to wait. And, everyone had guns.

I knew that during the civil war which began in 1975, that sometimes when a Muslim or Christian militiaman wanted to retaliate for the killing of one of his own, he would pull someone out of a car at a checkpoint and shoot him. I knew that it was dangerous, but I felt safe because I was an American and a woman. At that time they weren't killing women.

In 1983, I'd received my onward assignment – I was to go to Sri Lanka. I loved Beirut, but I was tired. It was April 18. I got to the embassy around noon and ran into Bob Pearson at the front door. He invited me down to the cafeteria for a farewell lunch. We were sitting near the back, watching people come in, when there was a loud noise – like a clap of thunder – and everything went black and silent, and I felt a shock through my whole body. My mind went through a lot of things; wondering if I was dead, and then thinking the whole thing was unfair, before I lost consciousness. I learned later what happened.

When the bomb detonated, the walls exploded outward, and I was blown out with them. Bob Pearson, oddly enough, wasn't. He was sitting next to me, and went up in the air and right back down, never losing consciousness. He told me later that he knew right away that it was a bomb. When I woke up, I couldn't move my arms because both of them were broken. I also had broken ribs and severed nerves, and I was covered with this white stuff that I thought at first was concrete. I lay there for a long time until I was finally rescued by four young men.

Of all the people in the cafeteria when the bomb exploded, Bob Pearson and I were the only ones to survive. The awful part is that they all died. You know, people talk about feeling guilty. I never felt guilty. I just felt terrible. I felt bad that they died and I didn't die. I always felt extraordinarily happy about being alive. I had a sense of joy that I had never experienced before. That lasted for almost a year. I wish I still had it.

Foreign Affairs Oral History Collection, Association for Diplomatic Studies and Training, Arlington, VA, www.adst.org.

Photographs of life in the diplomatic corps.

Photo Captions

(page 46)
Chinese soldiers who participated in the Boxer
Rebellion in 1900.
(public domain image)

A diplomatic passport does not
provide protection against violence.
(public domain image)

(page 47)
When disaffected Chinese attacked the foreign
Legation in Peiking in June 1900, laying siege
to the embassies there, over 200 foreigners – mostly
defenders – were killed. (public domain image)

A suicide truck bomb attack on the U.S. Embassy in
Beirut, Lebanon in 1983, caused 63 deaths, mostly
embassy and CIA staff members. (US Marine Corps
photo)

(page 48)
Mural outside the walls of the U.S. Embassy in
Teheran after it was taken over by student radicals.
(public domain image)

Celebrations after release of the Americans
held hostage in U.S. Embassy in Iran. (Faculty
Polytechnic.org photo)

(page 49)
Hole in the embassy compound wall through
which the Viet Cong infiltrated during the
Tet 1968 attack. (U.S. Army photograph)

Aftermath of the bombing of the U.S. Embassy in Dar es Salaam, Tanzania in 1998.
(U.S. Department of State photo)

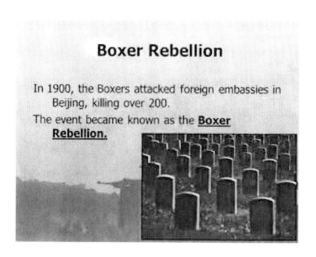

Appendix 1

Attacks on American Diplomatic Facilities

American embassies have been the target of attacks and bombings throughout the twentieth century, beginning with the siege of all foreign delegations in Peiking (now Beijing) during the Boxer Rebellion.

Date	Embassy/Consulate	Location	Deaths
1900	Foreign Legation Quarter (The Boxer Rebellion)	Peiking	68
May 1926	U.S. Embassy (Bombing)	Argentina	0
June 1926	U.S. Embassy (Bombing)	Uruguay	0
Mar. 1927	U.S. Embassy (Nanking Incident)	Nanking	0
July 1958	U.S. Embassy	Turkey	0

(Bombing)

Mar. 1964	U.S. Embassy (Bombing)	Gabon	0
Mar. 1965	U.S. Embassy (Bombing)	Vietnam	22
June 1967	U.S. Embassy (Attacked and burned)	Libya	0
Jan. 1968	U.S. Embassy (Tet '68 attack)	Vietnam	5
Sep. 1971	U.S. Embassy (Armed attack)	Cambodia	1
Feb. 1979	U.S. Embassy (Hostage taking)	Iran	0
Nov. 1979	U.S. Embassy (Hostile takeover)	Iran	9
Nov. 1979	U.S. Embassy (Burned)	Pakistan	4
Dec. 1979	U.S. Embassy (Burned)	Libya	0
Apr. 1983	U.S. Embassy (Bombing)	Lebanon	64
Dec. 1983	U.S. Embassy (Bombing)	Kuwait	6
Sep. 1984	U.S. Embassy	Lebanon	24

(Bombing)

Nov. 1984	U.S. Embassy (Bombing)	Colombia	1
May 1985	U.S. Embassy (Bombing)	Peru	0
1986	U.S. Embassy (Bombing)	Indonesia	0
1987	U.S. Embassy (Bombing)	Italy	0
1990	U.S. Embassy (Attack – failed)	Israel	0
Aug. 1998	U.S. Embassy (Bombing)	Kenya	212
Aug. 1998	U.S. Embassy (Bombing)	Tanzania	11
1999	U.S. Embassy (Mobs)	China	0
2002	American Center (Gunmen attack in Kolkata)	India	5
2002	U.S. Consulate (Gunmen attack in Karachi)	Pakistan	12
2004	U.S. Embassy (Bombing)	Uzbekistan	2
2004	U.S. Consulate	SaudiArabia	0

(Attack in Jeddah)

2006	U.S. Embassy (Bombing)	Syria	4
2007	U.S. Embassy (Attack)	Greece	0
2008	U.S. Embassy (Riot and protest)	Serbia	1
2008	U.S. Consulate (Attack in Istanbul)	Turkey	6
2008	U.S. Embassy (Attack)	Yemen	19
2010	U.S. Consulate (Bombing in Peshawar)	Pakistan	6
2011	U.S. Embassy (Civil War)	Syria	0
2011	U.S. Embassy (Attacks)	Afghanistan	0
2011	U.S. Embassy (Attacks)	Bosnia/Herzegovina	0
2012	U.S. Embassy (Attacks)	Egypt	0
2012	U.S. Consulate (Attack in Benghazi)	Libya	4
2012	U.S. Embassy	Yemen	0

(Attack)

2012	U.S. Embassy (Attack)	Tunisia	0
2013	U.S. Embassy (Bombing)	Turkey	2
Sep. 2013	U.S. Consulate (Attack in Herat)	Afghanistan	2

This list represents only attacks on American diplomatic facilities. During this same period, diplomatic facilities of scores of other nations were also attacked, bombed, or burned with often an even higher loss of life.

Appendix 2

The American Foreign Service Association
Memorial Plaque

The first American Foreign Service Association (AFSA) memorial plaque, which is located in the Diplomatic Lobby (on C Street) of the Department of State, was unveiled by Secretary of State Henry Stimson on March 3, 1933. The original plaque was at the entrance of what is now the Eisenhower Executive Office Building, next to the White House. At that time, what was known as the Executive Office Building (EOB) was home to the Departments of State and Navy. The inscription on that plaque reads, "Erected by members of the American Foreign Service Association in honor of diplomatic and consular officers of the United States who while on duty lost their lives under heroic or tragic circumstances." The plaque was limited to Foreign Service Officers until after World War II when all ranks were honored. In 1972, during the Vietnam War, the criteria were expanded to include Americans who 'served the country abroad in foreign affairs.' In 1982, the criteria were again expanded to include personnel of other agencies, including military, but this was changed in 2005 to exclude personnel whose agencies have their own memorials. The current criteria can be found on the AFSA Web site (www.afsa.org).

William Palfrey – Lost at Sea – 1780

Joel Barlow – Exposure – Zarnowice, 1812

Richard C. Anderson – Yellow Fever – Cartagena, Colombia, 1823

Nathaniel G. Ingraham, Jr. – Fever – Tampico, Mexico, 1824

Harris E. Fudger – Murdered – Bogota, Colombia, 1825

James A. Holden - Lost at Sea – 1832

John S. Meircken – Lost at Sea – 1832

William Shaler – Cholera – Havana, Cuba, 1833

William S. Sparks – Cholera – Venice, Italy, 1849

Thomas T. Turner – Epidemic – Bahia, 1849

Thomas I. Morgan – Yellow Fever – Rio De Janeiro, 1850

Hardy M. Burton – Yellow Fever – St. Thomas, 1852

George R. Dwyer – Coast Fever – Mozambique, 1854

Beverly L. Clarke – Tropical Fever – Guatemala, 1860

Isaac S. McMicken – Yellow Fever – Acapulco, Mexico, 1860

George True – Smallpox – Funchal, 1862

Edward W. Gardner – Lost at Sea – 1863

Charles G. Hannah – Yellow Fever – Demerara, 1864

Abraham Hanson – African Fever – Monrovia, Liberia, 1866

Hiram R. Hawkins – Epidemic – Tumbez, Peru, 1866

Allen A. Hall – Epidemic – La Paz, Bolivia, 1867

H. E. Peck – Yellow Fever – Haiti, 1867

James Wilson – Yellow Fever – Venezuela, 1867

James H. McColley – Yellow Fever – Callao, 1869

William Stedman – Yellow Fever – Santiago, Cuba, 1869

Charles E. Perry – Epidemic – Aspinwall, Colombia, 1872

Thomas Biddle – Epidemic – Guayaquil, 1875

John F. Flint – Drowned saving life – La Union, El Salvador, 1875

Philip Clayton – Yellow Fever – Callao, 1877

Henry H. Garnet – African Fever – Monrovia, 1882

Jesse H. Moore – Yellow Fever – Callao, 1883

David T. Bunker – Yellow Fever – Demerara, 1888

Victor F. W. Stanwood – Murdered – Madagascar, 1888

William D. McCoy – Fever – Monrovia, 1893

John R. Meade – Yellow Fever – Santo Domingo, 1894

Alexander L. Pollock – Yellow Fever – San Salvador, 1894

Frederick Munchmeyer – Yellow Fever – San Salvador, 1895

John B. Gorman – Malignant Malaria – Matamoros, Mexico, 1896

Albert S. Willis – Malaria – Honolulu, Hawaii, 1897

Rounsevelle Wildman – Lost at Sea – 1901

Thomas T. Prentis – Volcanic Eruption – Martinique, 1902

Amedee Testart – Volcanic Eruption – Martinique, 1902

Thomas Nast – Yellow Fever – Guayaquil, 1902

William F. Havemeyer – Cholera – Bassorah, Turkey, 1904

Philip Carroll – Fever – Manzanillo, Mexico, 1906

Benjamin H. Ridgely – Exhaustion – Mexico City, 1908

Arthur A. Cheney – Earthquake – Messina, 1908

John W. Gourley – Smallpox – Ciudad Juarez, Mexico, 1910

Theodore C. Hamm – Smallpox – Durango, Mexico, 1914

Robert N. McNeely – Lost at Sea – 1915

Charles P. McKiernan – Smallpox – Chungkiang, China, 1916

Charles F. Brissel – Cholera – Baghdad, 1916

Alfred L. M. Gottschalk – Lost at Sea – 1918

Maddin Summers - Exhaustion – Moscow, 1918

John D. O'Rear – Smallpox – La Paz, 1918

Luther K. Zabriskie – Smallpox – Aguas Calientes, Mexico, 1921

Carl R. Loop – Died Saving Life – Catania, 1923

Max D. Kirjassof – Earthquake – Yokohama, Japan, 1923

Paul E. Jenks – Earthquake – Yokohama, Japan, 1923

Clarence C. Woolard – Epidemic – Cape Haitien, Haiti, 1923

Robert W. Imbrie – Murdered – Tehran, Persia (now Iran), 1924

William T. Francis – Yellow Fever – Liberia, 1929

William I. Jackson – Drowned trying to save a life – Matanzas, Cuba, 1930

John T. Wainwright – Drowned trying to save a life – Matanzas, Cuba, 1930

G. Russell Taggart – Hurricane – Belize, British Honduras, 1931

J. Theodore Marriner – Murdered – Beirut, Syria, 1937

John M. Slaughter – Earthquake – Guayaquil, 1942

Thomas C. Wasson – Shot by Sniper – Jerusalem, 1948

Douglas S. Mackiernan – Killed by Gunfire – Tibet, 1950

Robert Lee Mikels – Died attempting to save a life – Pusan, Korea, 1951

David LeBreton, Jr. – Drowned saving lives – Tunis, 1953

William P. Boteler – Killed by Grenade – Nicosia, Cyprus, 1956

Robert A. McKinnon – Tropical Disease – Ouagadougou, 1961

Barbara A. Robbins – Killed in bombing of Embassy – Saigon, Vietnam, 1965

Joseph W. Grainger – Murdered – Vietnam, 1965

Joseph R. Rupley – Killed by Gunfire – Caracas, Venezuela, 1965

Dolph B. Owens – Cause of death not stated – Vietnam, 1960
Jack J. Wells – Plane crash – Vietnam, 1965

Norman L. Clowers – Viet Cong ambush – Vietnam, 1966

William D. Smith III – Cause of death not stated – Vietnam, 1966

Don M. Sjostrom – Cause of death not stated – Laos, 1967

John R. McLean – Cause of death not stated – Laos, 1967

Robert K. Franzblau – Shot while evacuating refugees – Vietnam, 1967

Dwight Hall Owen, Jr. – Killed by Communist forces – Vietnam, 1967

Carroll H. Pender – Landmine explosion – Vietnam, 1967

Frederick J. Abramson – Shot during Viet Cong ambush – Vietnam, 1968

Thomas M. Gompertz – Killed during Tet Offensive – Vietnam, 1968

John T. McCarthy – Died from gunshot wound – Vietnam, 1968

Kermit J. Krause – Killed during Tet Offensive – Vietnam, 1968

Jeffrey S. Lundstedt – Killed during Tet Offensive – Vietnam, 1968

Robert R. Little – Killed during Tet Offensive – Vietnam, 1968

Stephen H. Miller – Cause of death not stated – Vietnam, 1968

Hugh C. Lobit – Shot by sniper – Vietnam, 1968

Richard A. Schenk – Landmine explosion – Vietnam, 1968

Michael Murphy – Viet Cong ambush – Vietnam, 1968

John Gordon Mein – Shot by Guatemalen rebels – Guatemala, 1968

George B. Gaines – Died from gunshot wounds – Vietnam, 1969

Robert P. Perry – Murdered by Palestinian terrorists - Jordan, 1970

Dan A. Mitrione – Assassinated by Uruguayan rebels – Uruguay, 1970

Cleo Allen Noel, Jr. – Assassinated by Palestinian terrorists – Sudan, 1973

George Curtis Moore – Assassinated by Palestinian terroritst – Sudan, 1973

Everett D. Reese – Killed in action – Vietnam, 1955

Thomas W. Ragsdale – Died while a prisoner of war – Vietnam, 1967

Donald V. Freeman – Shot during hostile fire – Vietnam, 1967

Albert A. Farkas – Pulmonary embolism after sniper wound – Vietnam, 1968

Robert W. Brown, Jr. – Shot during hostile fire – Vietnam, 1968

Robert W. Hubbard – Killed while trying to escape from Viet Cong – Vietnam, 1968

Joseph B. Smith – Landmine explosion – Vietnam, 1970

Rudolph Kaiser – Viet Cong ambush – Vietnam, 1972

John Paul Vann – Helicopter crash – Vietnam, 1972

John S. Patterson – Kidnapped and murdered – Mexico, 1974

Rodger P. Davies – Shot by sniper – Cyprus, 1974

James C. Marshall – Killed during Tet Offensive – Vietnam, 1968

Steven A. Haukness - Killed during Tet Offensive – Vietnam, 1968

Charles W. Turberville – Killed in bomb blast – Cambodia, 1971

John Patrick Egan – Kidnapped and killed by insurgents – Argentina, 1975

Charles McMahon – Rocket attack – Vietnam, 1975

Darwin L. Judge – Rocket attack – Vietnam, 1975

Thomas Olmstead – Pancreatitis – Cambodia, 1975

Francis E. Meloy, Jr. – Assassinated by terrorists – Beirut, Lebanon, 1976

Robert O. Waring – Assassinated by terrorists – Beirut, Lebanon, 1976

Adolph Dubs – Kidnapped and killed by terrorists – Kabul, 1979

Steven J. Crowley – Shot by mob – Islamabad, 1979

Bryan L. Ellis – Died attempting to save life – Islamabad, 1979

Charles Robert Ray – Assassinated by terrorists – Paris, 1982

Robert C. Ames – Killed in bombing of Embassy – Beirut, 1983

Thomas R. Blacka – Killed in bombing of Embassy –

Beirut, 1983

Phyliss N. Faraci – Killed in bombing of Embassy – Beirut, 1983

Terry L. Gilden – Killed in bombing of Embassy – Beirut, 1983

Kenneth E. Haas – Killed in bombing of Embassy – Beirut, 1983

Deborah M. Hixon – Killed in bombing of Embassy – Beirut, 1983

Frank J. Johnston – Killed in bombing of Embassy – Beirut, 1983

James F. Lewis – Killed in bombing of Embassy – Beirut, 1983

Monique Lewis – Killed in bombing of Embassy – Beirut, 1983

William R. McIntyre – Killed in bombing of Embassy – Beirut, 1983

Robert V. McMaugh – Killed in bombing of Embassy – Beirut, 1983

William R. Sheil – Killed in bombing of Embassy – Beirut, 1983

Albert N. Votaw – Killed in bombing of Embassy – Beirut, 1983

George Tsantes – Killed by gunshot – Athens, 1983

Leamon R. Hunt – Murdered by guerillas – Rome, 1984

Kenneth G. Crabtree – Killed in bombing – Namibia, 1984

Dennis Whyte Keogh – Killed in bombing – Namibia, 1984

A.A. Schaufelberger III – Shot by insurgents – San Salvador, 1983

Charles F. Soper – Cause of death not stated – New Delhi, 1983

Michael Ray Wagner – Killed in bombing of Embassy – Beirut, 1984

Kenneth V. Welch – Killed in bombing of Embassy – Beirut, 1984

Charles F. Hegna – Killed by gunmen on plane – Tehran, Iran, 1984

William L. Stanford – Killed by gunmen on plane – Tehran, Iran, 1984

Enrique Camarena – Killed by drug traffickers – Guadalajara, 1985

Virginia Warfield - Automobile accident – New Delhi, 1983

Bobby Joe Dickson – Shot – San Salvador, 1985

Thomas T. Handwork – Shot – San Salvador, 1985

Patrick R. Kwiatkowski – Shot – San Salvador, 1985

Gregory H. Weber – Shot – San Salvador, 1985

Laurence A. Steinhardt – Plane crash – Ottawa, Canada, 1950

William F. Buckley – Kidnapped and killed by terrorists – Beirut, 1985

William E. Nordeen – Car bombing – Athens, 1988

Arnold L. Raphel – Aircraft explosion – Pakistan, 1988

Herbert M. Wassom – Aircraft explosion – Pakistan, 1988

Matthew K. Gannon – Airplane bombing – Scotland, 1988

Ronald A. Lariviere – Airplane bombing – Scotland, 1988

Daniel E. O'Conner – Airplane bombing – Scotland, 1988

James N. Rowe – Shot by Communists – Philippines, 1989

John A. Butler – Shot in crossfire – Grenada, 1989

Gladys D. Gilbert – Plane crash – Ethiopia, 1989

Robert W. Woods – Plane crash – Ethiopia, 1989

Thomas J. Worrick – Plane crash – Ethiopia, 1989

Freddie R. Woodruff – Drive-by shooting – Republic of Georgia, 1993

Barbara L. Schell – Helicopter crash – Iraq, 1994

Barry S. Castiglione – Died during ocean rescue – El Salvador, 1992

Jacqueline K. Van Landingham – Ambushed by terrorists – Pakistan, 1995

Gary C. Durell – Ambushed by terrorists – Pakistan, 1995

Samuel Nelson Drew – Automobile accident – Bosnia, 1995

Robert C. Frasure – Automobile accident – Bosnia, 1995

Joseph J. Kruzel – Automobile accident – Bosnia, 1995

Ronald H. Brown – Plane crash – Croatia, 1996

Lee F. Jackson – Plane crash – Croatia, 1996

Stephen C. Kaminski – Plane crash – Croatia, 1996

Leslianne Shedd – Plane crash – Comoros, 1996
Nathan Aliganga – Embassy bombing – Kenya, 1998

Julian Leotis Bartley, Sr. – Embassy bombing – Kenya, 1998

Molly Huckaby Hardy – Embassy bombing – Kenya, 1998

Kenneth R. Hobson II – Embassy bombing – Kenya, 1998

Prabhi G. Kavaler – Embassy bombing – Kenya, 1998

Michelle O'Connor – Embassy bombing – Kenya, 1998

Sherry Lynn Olds – Embassy bombing – Kenya, 1998

Uttamlal Tom Shah – Embassy bombing, Kenya, 1998

Seth John Foti – Plane crash – Bahrain, 2000

Philip Thomas Lincoln, Jr. – Automobile accident – China, 1996

J. Kirby Simon – Carbon Monoxide poisoning – Taiwan, 1995

Nancy Ferebee Lewis – Pesticide poisoning – Egypt, 1993

Pasqual Martine - Hotel fire – Russia, 1991

Robert B. Hebb – Plane crash – Honduras, 1989

Edward R. Cheney – Plane crash – Philippines, 1976

Garnett A. Zimmerly – Plane crash – Philippines, 1976

Bruce O. Bailey – Plane crash – Vietnam, 1972

Luther A. McLendon, Jr. – Plane crash – Vietnam,

1972

Livingston Lord Satterthwaite – Helicopter crash – Greenland, 1959

William Dale Fisher – Plane crash – Ethiopia, 1961

Gustav Crane Hertz – Died of malaria while in captivity – Vietnam, 1967

Rose Marie Orlich – Earthquake – Nicaragua, 1972

Richard Aitken – Automobile accident – Sudan, 1981

Philip Robert Hanson – Plane crash – Togo, 1981

James David Marill – Automobile accident – Cameroon, 1986

Rebecca Roberts – Carbon Monoxide poisoning – Israel, 1987

Marie D. Burke – Murdered – United Kingdom, 1989

Thomas P. Doubleday, Jr. – Malaria – Liberia, 1993

James T. Lederman – Automobile accident – Egypt, 1994

Barbara J. Green – Terrorist attack – Pakistan, 2002

Laurence M. Foley – Terrorist attack – Jordan, 2002

Jerry V. Cook – Automobile accident – Madagascar, 1978

Richard A. Coulter – Automobile accident – Iran,

1975

Howard V. Funk, Jr. – Automobile accident – Kenya, 1972

Oscar C. Holder – Plane crash – Nepal, 1962

Sidney B. Jacques – Plane crash – Nepal, 1962

James Mollen – Terrorist attack – Iraq, 2004

Edward J. Seitz – Rocket attack – Iraq, 2004

John Francis O'Grady – Plane crash – Australia, 1960

Barbara C. Heald – Rocket attack – Iraq, 2005

Keith E. Taylor – Rocket attack – Iraq, 2005

Stephen E. Sullivan – Terrorist attack – Iraq, 2005

David E. Foy – Terrorist attack – Pakistan, 2006

Margaret Alexander – Helicopter crash – Nepal, 2006

Doris Knittle – Murdered – Afghanistan, 1970

Henry W. Antheil, Jr. – Plane explosion – Estonia, 1940

Steven Thomas Stefani, IV – Killed by bomb – Afghanistan, 2007

John Michael Granville – Vehicle ambush – Sudan, 2008

Brian Daniel Adkins – Murdered – Ethiopia, 2009

Felix Russell Engdahl – Died from accidental fall in POW Camp – Hong Kong, 1942

Thomas W. Waldron – Cholera – Macau, 1844

Edmund Roberts – Dysentery – Macau, 1844

Victoria J. DeLong – Earthquake – Haiti, 2010

Dale J. Gredler – Heart attack – Indonesia, 2010

Terrence L. Barnich – Roadside bomb – Iraq, 2009

Eugene F. Sullivan – Black Water Fever – Ethiopia, 1972

Sharon S. Clarke – Cerebral Malaria – Nigeria, 2010

Francis J. Savage – Viet Cong bombing – Vietnam, 1967

Joseph Gregory Fandino – Cause of death not stated – Vietnam, 1972

Ragaei Said Abdelfattah – Cause of death not stated – Afghanistan, 2012

Glen A. Doherty - Terrorist attack – Libya, 2012

Ty Woods – Terrorist attack – Libya, 2012

Sean Patrick Smith – Terrorist attach – Libya, 2012

J. Christopher Stevens – Terrorist attack – Libya, 2012

Anne T. Smedinghoff – Terrorist attack – Afghanistan, 2013

Antoinette Beaumont Tomasek – Automobile accident – Haiti, 2013

Editor's note: Names are listed here in the order they were added to the plaque rather than the date of death or incident. For flow and consistency, some entries have been edited – but the meaning or essential content has not been changed.

Appendix 3

Bibliography

Burton, Fred and Katz, Samuel. *Under Fire.* London: Icon Books, 2014.

Dorman, Shawn, ed. *Inside a U.S. Embassy: Diplomacy at Work.* Washington, DC: Foreign Service Books, 2011.

Hevener, Natalie Kaufman, ed. *Diplomacy in a Dangerous World: Protection for Diplomats Under International Law.* Boulder, CO: Westview Press, 1986.

Hill, Christopher R. *Outpost: Life on the Frontlines of American Diplomacy.* New York: Simon and Schuster, 2014.

Keeley, Robert V., ed. *First Line of Defense: Ambassadors, Embassies and American Interests Abroad.* Washington, DC: American Academy of Diplomacy, 2000.

Kopp, Harry W. *Career Diplomacy: Life and Work in the U.S. Foreign Service.* Washington, DC: Georgetown University Press, 2011.

Kralev, Nicholas. *America's Other Army: The U.S. Foreign Service and 21st Century Diplomacy.* Washington, DC: CreateSpace, 2012.

Larson, Erik. *In the Garden of Beasts: Love, Terror, and an American Family in Hitler's Berlin.* New York: Random House, 2011.

Mak, Dayton, and Charles Stuart Kennedy. *American Ambassadors in a Troubled World: Interviews with Senior Diplomats.* Westwood, CT: Greenwood Press, 1992.

Appendix 4

Glossary and Abbreviations

AC-130: The C-130 Hercules transport plane, the workhorse of the U.S. Air Force, is built by Lockheed. The AC-130 is a heavily armed ground attack version of the C-130, which is an airframe built by Lockheed which was converted to a gunship by Boeing for use during the Vietnam War to replace AC-47, which was a conversion of a WWII transport aircraft.

AFSA: The American Foreign Service Association is the professional association and bargaining unit for members of the U.S. Foreign Service of the Departments of State, Commerce, Agriculture, USAID, and the Broadcasting Board of Governors.

Aide-de-camp: The personal assistant to a senior official, most often a military or naval officer of general or flag rank.

AK-47: A selective-fire, gas-operated 7.62 x 39 mm

assault rifle, developed in the Soviet Union by Mikhail Kalashnikov during the final year of WWII. It was introduced into the Soviet Army in 1948, and has since become one of the most widely manufactured and used weapons in the world.

ARSO: Assistant Regional Security Officer. An embassy or consulate official working under the supervision of a Regional Security Officer (RSO) who is responsible for personnel and physical security of the organization.

Attaché: A specialist assigned (attached) to a diplomatic mission, e.g. military attaché, legal attaché.

Boxers: A name that foreigners gave to a Chinese secret society known as the Yihequan (Righteous and Harmonious Fists), whose aim was the destruction of the Qing Dynasty and the removal of Western influence from China.

CH-53: A heavy-lift helicopter used by the U.S. Marine Corps, the CH-53 is made by Sikorsky. The largest military helicopter, it is used to transport equipment, vehicles, combat-loaded Marines, or in humanitarian operations such as noncombatant evacuations.

Concertina wire: A type of barbed or razor wire that comes in large coils and can be expanded like a concertina.

Consulate: A constituent or subordinate post under an embassy, located outside the capital of a country.

Consulate General: Similar to a consulate, only located in larger cities or covering a large geographic area of a country outside the capital.

Corniche: A road that winds alongside a steep coast or cliff.

DATT: Defense Attaché. A military official assigned (attached) to an embassy. Part of the country team under the authority of the ambassador or chief of mission, the DATT also works for the Defense Intelligence Agency (DIA) and the geographic combatant command commander in whose area of operation the embassy is located.

DCM: Deputy Chief of Mission. The number two official in an embassy. In an American embassy, the DCM is the senior Department of State official. In addition to being in charge of the mission in the ambassador's absence from country, the DCM also manages internal embassy operations.

EAC: Emergency Action Committee. A team of embassy officials chaired by the DCM who are responsible for managing crises in the country of assignment.

FBI: Federal Bureau of Investigation. FBI or Justice Department personnel in an embassy are legal attachés.

FSI: Foreign Service Institute. The State Department's training institution where department employees and other foreign affairs agency personnel can get training in languages, area studies, and other subjects relating to serving overseas.

FSN: Foreign Service National (See LES).

Fulbright Program: A program of highly competitive, merit-based grants for international educational exchange, founded by Senator J. William Fulbright in 1946.

GPU: Ground power unit. Used to power aircraft when they are parked on the ground.

Helo: Idiomatic or slang term for a helicopter.

Junior officer: An officer of the U.S. Foreign Service in the lower ranks (normally FS-05 and below). In the Foreign Service, the lower number (i.e., FS-01) indicates a higher rank.

LAV: Light armored vehicle.

LES: Locally Employed Staff (formerly Foreign Service National) are the employees of diplomatic or consular missions in the country of assignment (usually citizens of that country).

MACV: Military Assistance Command – Vietnam. The military headquarters responsible for prosecuting the Vietnam War. MACV headquarters was located in Saigon near Tan Son Nhut Air Base (now Tan Son Nhut International Airport).

NEO: Noncombatant Evacuation Operation. The evacuation of civilian government employees and private citizens from an area of danger.

NVA: North Vietnamese Army.

OPSCO: Operations Coordinator. The senior enlisted person in the Defense Attaché Office.

Ordered Departure: A situation when all personnel of a diplomatic mission are required by their government to depart their country of assignment for security reasons.

PAO: Public Affairs Officer. Responsible for public relations, media affairs, and cultural programs of a diplomatic mission.

PJ: This is a term that has two meanings for most government people. In this book, it stands for pajamas. But, it is also a term used to refer to U.S. Air Force pararescuemen (para-jumpers) who conduct search and rescue or personnel recovery operations.

R & R: Rest and Recuperation. Official vacation time for employees (military or civilian) stationed overseas.

RSO: Regional Security Officer. The official at an embassy or consulate responsible for personnel and physical security.

SAS: A unit of the British army founded in 1941, which conducts reconnaissance, counter-terrorism, and other special operations.

SF: Special Forces.

State: Shorthand reference to the U.S. Department of State – used primarily by personnel assigned to the Department.

TDY: Temporary duty. Assigned duty away from an individual's normal place of work.

UN: United Nations.

USAID: U.S. Agency for International Development. The agency responsible for implementation of U.S. foreign aid programs abroad.

USG: An abbreviation for United States Government.

USIS: United States Information Service. Before it was folded into the Department of State in 1999, the United States Information Agency (USIA) was known as USIS when overseas to avoid confusion with the Central Intelligence Agency (CIA).

Yihetuan: Righteous and Harmonious Fists. A Chinese secret society organized to overthrow the Qing dynasty and drive foreigners out of China. See **Boxers**.

A Note from the Editor

I have long been a student of history, and after retiring from a 30-year career in the U.S. Foreign Service (preceded by 20 years in the U.S. Army), I decided that I wanted to fill the gaps I've seen in the knowledge most Americans have about what American diplomats do, in particular the perils they face daily as they work to protect the interests of the country and its citizens in some of the most dangerous places on earth.

Shortly after my retirement in 2012 I issued a public call for stories from those who have served – past and present. During my career, I learned that most people in this profession tend to shy away from publicity, so I wasn't completely surprised at the low response to my request for stories of the dangers American diplomats face.

This is a short book – for two reasons. One I've just mentioned; it's difficult to get Foreign Service people to talk publicly about what they do. Those that did, though, did – I sincerely believe – a great job of it. The variety of the stories in this small volume tell a much larger story, and I do believe give a fulsome picture of what it's like to serve as an American diplomat in a very dangerous world.

There are many more stories out there, and I hope that one day more of them can be told. In the meantime, if you've liked this brief introduction, it would be great if you would leave a review on amazon.com or any other book review site that you have access to. If you're a blogger, mentioning it on your blog would also be appreciated.

If there are any questions or comments you'd rather provide to me directly, I can be contacted at charlesray.author@gmail.com.

About the Editor

Charles Ray joined the U.S. Foreign Service in 1982, after completing 20 years of service in the U.S. Army. As a Foreign Service Officer he served overseas in China, Thailand, Sierra Leone, Vietnam, Cambodia, and Zimbabwe, and in the U.S. in the State Department's Bureau of Politico-Military Affairs, as diplomat-in-residence at the University of Houston, and as Deputy Assistant Secretary of Defense for POW/Missing Personnel Affairs.

His overseas tours were in consular affairs and management. He was the deputy chief of mission in Freetown, Sierra Leone during that country's civil war and transition to elected civilian government (1993-1996); the first U.S. consul general in Ho Chi Minh City (formerly Saigon), Vietnam (1998-2001); ambassador to the Kingdom of Cambodia (2002-2005); and ambassador to Zimbabwe (2009-2012). He retired from the Foreign Service in 2012. A member of the American Foreign Service Association (AFSA), he was the first chair of AFSA's Committee on the Foreign Service Profession and Ethics, and he is a member of the American Academy of Diplomacy and the Association of Black American Ambassadors.

He is currently engaged in writing, consulting and

lecturing. In 2014 he conducted a workshop on professional writing for Rangel Scholars at Howard University in Washington, DC, and lectures occasionally at the Osher Lifelong Learning Institute of Johns Hopkins University. He has written more than 40 books of fiction and nonfiction, including four books on leadership and management.

A native of Texas, he currently resides in Montgomery County, Maryland, just outside Washington, DC.

CPSIA information can be obtained at www.ICGtesting.com
Printed in the USA
BVOW01s1246090115

382690BV00004B/11/P